INDECENT

BOOKS BY PAULA VOGEL
AVAILABLE FROM TCG

The Baltimore Waltz and Other Plays

INCLUDES:

The Baltimore Waltz
And Baby Makes Seven
Desdemona
Hot 'N' Throbbing
The Oldest Profession

A Civil War Christmas: An American Musical Celebration

How I Learned to Drive

Indecent

The Long Christmas Ride Home

The Mammary Plays

INCLUDES:

How I Learned to Drive
The Mineola Twins

"Heart-stirring and haunting . . . A dramatic reminder of the power of art." —NEW YORK DAILY NEWS

"An exhilarating ride . . . *Indecent* is a fantastic work of imagination, craft and history, seamlessly interweaving a forgotten play—and the tragic history of that forgotten play—into a spellbinding evening." —DEADLINE

"A marvelous play. *Indecent* melds fact and fiction with the kind of insight and emotional depth that comes from theater at its most poetic." —NYI

"A riveting drama." —VARIETY

"A tender, unconventional play . . . An original and vibrant approach, *Indecent* is a project of reclamation, an homage and a recuperation of a text that had its cultural moment and then vanished almost entirely. *Indecent* has tremendous affection for the whole of the play and makes you long for the scenes . . . exquisite." —GUARDIAN

"A fascinating theatrical tale, *Indecent* exerts an undeniable power." —HOLLYWOOD REPORTER

"*Indecent* reminds us of the power of art to tell us truths long before we are able to recognize them as such." —LOS ANGELES TIMES

"Love of art, truth, same-sex partners, as well as the persecution of artists and the Jews aren't exactly underplayed themes in theater. But, oh, how deftly Paula Vogel crafts them into *Indecent* . . . Replete with freshness and vitality, *Indecent* is earnest without sentimentality, embraceable without solicitation, and inspiring without didacticism." —NEW HAVEN REGISTER

INDECENT

A PLAY BY

PAULA VOGEL

THEATRE COMMUNICATIONS GROUP
NEW YORK
2017

Indecent is published by Theatre Communications Group, Inc., 520 Eighth Avenue, 24th Floor, New York, NY 10018-4156

The publication of *Indecent* by Paula Vogel, through TCG's Book Program, is made possible in part by the New York State Council on the Arts with the support of Governor Andrew Cuomo and the New York State Legislature.

Special thanks to Paula Marie Black for her generous support of this publication.

TCG books are exclusively distributed to the book trade by Consortium Book Sales and Distribution.

Library of Congress Control Numbers:
2017010828 (print) / 2017014472 (ebook)
ISBN 978-1-55936-547-5 (softcover) / ISBN 978-1-55936-868-1 (ebook)
A catalog record for this book is available from the Library of Congress.

Book design and composition by Lisa Govan
Cover design by Monet Cogbill
Cover photograph: Adina Verson (left) and Katrina Lenk from the Vineyard Theatre production of *Indecent*. Photograph copyright © 2017 by Carol Rosegg.

First Edition, November 2017
Sixth Printing, October 2020

PREFACE

I got the phone call sometime in 2009. Rebecca Taichman was calling from Ashland, Oregon: Would I be interested in writing a play about the infamous 1923 obscenity trial of Sholem Asch's *The God of Vengeance*?

I had read the play in the stacks at Cornell University my first year in grad school; the love scene between two women written by a twenty-something-year-old newly married man stunned me. Moreover, he had written the play in 1906. It left an indelible impression on my twenty-two-year-old mind, and I would never again make assumptions that the gender of the writer determined the empathic understanding of gender.

And when my brother gave me, as his last gift, the book *We Can Always Call Them Bulgarians*, I read about the trial. And promptly filed away the incident until I read about a young director in graduate school who staged the obscenity trial as her thesis: "The People vs. *The God of Vengeance*" in 2000.

Who is this woman? I began to track her work. And every play she directed was stunning.

I hoped I would work with her.

Then, the phone call. Would I be interested in writing a play about the trial, Rebecca asked. She had realized that she could not work out her obsession by using found materials; she would need a writer.

I had briefly dallied with writing a play about the trial of *The Well of Loneliness*, and Mae West's *The Drag*. But perhaps it was the inspiration to me that this brilliant woman had held on to this story, which suddenly gave me a vision. This is how, for me, plays happen. I see an image that ends up being the turning point: a woman adjusts her car mirror. A doctor takes off his latex gloves under fluorescent hospital lights, or:

A dusty troupe of actors hastily assemble a performance of *The God of Vengeance* with improvised props and suitcases and trunks in an attic.

I asked the other voice on the line: "I think it's larger than the obscenity trial." And Rebecca gave me an enthusiastic: "Yes, yes! You should make it what you want!"

And from that call followed perhaps the most extended and intimate collaboration of my life. She unearthed a box of materials from her thesis: the entire trial transcript, letters from the producer Harry Weinberger, her thesis itself.

And then I read. We went to MacDowell together, and she typed from dictation in the cabin we shared; every day we would stop and Rebecca would play the roles and read the pages. And we would discuss every page.

We emerged with the first draft in two weeks. A not very good first draft, but still, the block of marble I could carve to find the marble elephant within.

Workshops. A week at her parents' house, Ettie and Lazer Taichman, where I consumed more books from her parents' shelves. A week at my house in Rhode Island, a week at the Cape. Three weeks at Sundance Theatre Lab. A reading here, another workshop there . . . Only with the generosity of multiple not-for-profits: Sundance, Yale Repertory Theatre, La Jolla Playhouse (and her initial commission from Oregon Shakespeare Festival joined my commission at Yale) could we put together a troupe to make it happen.

Ultimately, I discarded the obscenity trial from the play. We entered into the collaboration with Rebecca's dream of me writing that play. But it didn't fit, and I couldn't make it fit. Over the next seven years of reading about Łódź, Yiddish theater, the history of the Lower East Side, theses about theater in the camps and ghettos, and listening to music and more music, I slowly carved out the play. For every scene in the play, there are scenes on the cutting room floor. For every character in the play, there were multiple rewrites.

And somehow, as I wrote, I fell in love with this world until my obsession matched my director's. I jettisoned other projects, choosing to stay at home with my research, listening at the end of every day to a recording of "Wiegela," and weeping at Ilse Weber's haunting lullaby.

With a brilliant director, two co-composers, Aaron Halva and Lisa Gutkin, and the generous spirit of choreographer David Dorfman, I could write a tour of Europe in a page, with four repetitions of a scene, and hand it over to Rebecca: "What do I do with this?" she asked. "Your problem! Have fun!" I said. And have fun she did. Make a dead troupe rise from the ashes? She came up with the idea of the dust. End with a stunning rain scene? Through three productions we tried variations until it worked. She staged my intention with more life than I could ever dictate through stage directions alone. And of course, along the way, the same brilliant cast, composers and choreographer stayed with us, with suggestions and ideas that brought the play to life.

There are storied collaborations in the American Theater, writer/director collaborations that over years result in plays that remain vivid on the page: Elia Kazan and Tennessee Williams. Lloyd Richards and August Wilson. Marshall Mason and Lanford Wilson.

Rebecca Taichman and our troupe put my voice on the stage. I can only hope that these pages inspire more rich collaborations in our theater.

This play is dedicated to Rebecca Taichman's immigrant ancestors. And mine. And all of ours.

Paula Vogel
Wellfleet, MA
May 2017

Indecent

Original Broadway Production
Conceived and Directed by Rebecca Taichman

Indecent was co-commissioned by Oregon Shakespeare Festival (Bill Rauch, Artistic Director; Cynthia Rider, Executive Director) in Ashland, OR, as part of their American Revolutions: The United States History Cycle, and Yale Repertory Theatre (James Bundy, Artistic Director; Victoria Nolan, Managing Director) in New Haven, CT.

Indecent received its world premiere in a co-production of Yale Repertory Theatre and La Jolla Playhouse (Christopher Ashley, Artistic Director; Michael S. Rosenberg, Managing Director) in La Jolla, CA. It opened at Yale Repertory Theatre on October 2, 2015, and at La Jolla Playhouse on November 13, 2015. The production was conceived and directed by Rebecca Taichman. The scenic design was by Riccardo Hernandez, the costume design was by Emily Rebholz, the lighting design was by Christopher Akerlind, the original music was by Lisa Gutkin and Aaron Halva, the sound design was by Matt Hubbs, the projection design was by Tal Yarden, the choreography was by David Dorfman; the production stage manager was Amanda Spooner. The cast was:

LEMML, THE STAGE MANAGER	Richard Topol
THE ACTORS	Katrina Lenk, Mimi Lieber, Max Gordon Moore, Tom Nelis, Steven Rattazzi, Adina Verson

THE MUSICIANS   Lisa Gutkin, Aaron Halva,
                       Travis W. Hendrix

Indecent had its New York premiere at Vineyard Theatre (Douglas Aibel and Sarah Stern, Co-Artistic Directors; Suzanne Appel, Managing Director) on April 27, 2016. The cast and creative team remained the same as the Yale Rep/La Jolla production, with the following changes: Mike Cohen replaced Travis W. Hendrix as a Musician, and the production stage manager was Terri K. Kohler.

Indecent opened on Broadway at the Cort Theatre on April 18, 2017. The producers were Daryl Roth, Elizabeth I. McCann, Cody Lassen, Jerry Meyer, Jay Alix & Una Jackman, Elizabeth Armstrong, Julie Boardman, CoGro Partners, Nicole Eisenberg, Four Star Productions, GLS Productions, The John Gore Organization, Kathleen K. Johnson, Dana M. Lerner, Jenn Maley, Mano-Horn Productions, Marc Platt, and Storyboard Entertainment. The cast and creative team remained the same as the Vineyard production, with the following changes: Matt Darriau replaced Mike Cohen as a Musician, and the production stage manager was James Latus.

CHARACTERS

The Dead Troupe. The Troupe plays everyone.

The Troupe

THE STAGE MANAGER, LEMML

The Ingenue (Chana)

RIFKELE

MADJE ASCH

ELSA HEIMES

IMMIGRANT

REINA/RUTH

VIRGINIA MCFADDEN

BAGELMAN SISTER

The Ingenue (Avram)

SHOLEM ASCH

IMMIGRANT

MORRIS CARNOVSKY

EUGENE O'NEILL

JOHN ROSEN

The Middle (Halina)

MANKE

IMMIGRANT

FREIDA NIEMANN

DEINE/DOROTHEE

DR. HORNIG

BAGELMAN SISTER

The Middle (Mendel)

NAKHMEN

IMMIGRANT

HARRY WEINBERGER

OFFICER BENJAMIN BAILIE

RABBI JOSEPH SILVERMAN

The Elder (Vera)	*The Elder (Otto)*
SARAH	YEKEL
MRS. PERETZ	MR. PERETZ
IMMIGRANT	RUDOLPH SCHILDKRAUT
ESTHER STOCKTON	IMMIGRANT
MADJE ASCH	BARTENDER
	JUDGE MCINTYRE
	SCHOLEM ASCH

The Musicians

MAYER BALSAM, CLARINET, ISAAC

NELLY FRIEDMAN, VIOLIN

MORIZ GODOWSKY, ACCORDION, LAZAR

PLACE

Warsaw, 1906, to Bridgeport, Connecticut, 1950s, and everywhere in between.

SET

A space filled with planks and suitcases. All props come from the suitcases.

TITLES

Scene titles and Yiddish translations are projected throughout the production. In this publication they look like: FROM ASHES THEY RISE *or* IN YIDDISH: *etc.*

LANGUAGE

When characters speak their native language, they speak perfect English (when Sholem Asch, Madja Asch speak Yiddish, for example). When characters speak English as their second language, they speak in a dialect (Reine, Madja, Esther, and Asch, for example; Rudolph Schildkraut has the most intense dialect in America).

NOTE

An "/" indicates when dialogue overlaps.

INDECENT: THE TRUE STORY OF A LITTLE JEWISH PLAY

Lights up. Soft, muffled music.
Slowly, in a dim light, a body stirs onstage. The light grows; we see a dusty figure in an old suit. He stretches limbs that haven't moved in decades. He lifts one arm; sawdust pours from his sleeve. He lifts the other arm; more sawdust. He shakes his legs vigorously; more out-pouring of sawdust.

FROM ASHES THEY RISE

The troupe rises and shakes off their dust.
Lemml steps on the platform.

LEMML INTRODUCES THE TROUPE

LEMML: Ladies and gentlemen. Our actors who play many, many, roles tonight! First, the founding members of our

9

troupe. Vera Parnicki and Otto Godowsky. They play all of the fathers, all of the mothers, the sagest of our characters, or the ones who remain fools at any age.

(The man and woman acknowledge the audience.)

And our members of the troupe who are in their prime! Halina Cygansky and Mendel Schultz! They play all of the vamps and all of the vice, the scarred, and the schemers.

And our ingenues! Chana Mandelbaum and Avram Zederbaum. All the brides, all the grooms, the writers, the socialists. So ardent in their beliefs, so passionate in their lovemaking.

On violin: *Nelly Friedman! (She steps forward)*
On clarinet: *Mayer Balsam! (He does the same)*
And on accordion: *Moriz Godowsky. (He gives a wave)*

My name is Lemml; you can also call me Lou. I'm the stage manager tonight—usually you can find me backstage. We have a story we want to tell you . . . About a play. A play that changed my life. Every night we tell this story—but somehow I can never remember the end. *(He indicates his mind is failing. He turns to the others for help. No one can)* No matter. I can remember how it begins. It all starts with this moment—remember this:

(Lemml gestures to two women of the troupe, holding each other, and then the troupe explodes in a joyous klezmer song and dance.)

"ALE BRIDER"

(The cast sings "Ale Brider":)

CAST:

Oy yoy yoy yoy de yoy . . .

OTTO, MENDEL AND AVRAM:
  Un mir zaynen ale brider,
    oy, oy ale brider   *(We are all brothers*
  Un mit zingen freylekhe lider,
    oy oy oy.   *We sing happy songs.)*

VERA, HALINA AND CHANA:
  Un mir haltn zikh in eynem,
    oy oy zikh in eynem   *(We stick together*
  Azelkes iz nito bay keynem,
    oy oy oy!   *Like nobody does!)*

CAST:
  Oy yoy yoy yoy de yoy . . .

(Band solo.)

  Oy yoy yoy yoy de yoy . . .

(Members of the troupe form a bed from suitcases and planks. A young woman gets into the bed and waits. The troupe now brings a young man to the bed to join his young bride. Lemml takes a script from a suitcase and puts it in the bride's hands. The troupe gathers around the bed and watches the young woman read.)

1906, WARSAW: MADJE ASCH READS
THE GOD OF VENGEANCE IN BED WITH SHOLEM ASCH

Sholem Asch, a twenty-three-year-old playwright, waits as his wife reads the last page of The God of Vengeance.

IN YIDDISH:

MADJE: OH!! (*Reads a little further*)
ASCH: Oh???
MADJE: Ohhh . . .
ASCH: Ohhh as in it's awful??? Oh as in how do I tell him? Oh as in whom did I marry?

(*Madje reads. End of play.*
    Madje puts the manuscript down on her breasts. She closes her eyes. She opens her eyes. She inhales. She weeps.)

MADJE: Ohhh!
ASCH: Are you crying?
MADJE: I can't breathe.
    Oh as in it's wonderful. It's so sad. I love it.
ASCH: Really?
MADJE: Really.
ASCH: What did you love?
MADJE: My God, Sholem. It's all in there. The roots of all evil: the money, the subjugation of women, the false piety . . . the terrifying violence of that father . . . and then, oh Sholem, the two girls in the rain scene! My God, the poetry in it—what is it about your writing that makes me hold my breath? You make me feel the desire between these two women is the purest, most chaste, most spiritual—
ASCH: —It is! . . . are you angry? That I stole your words for the virgin daughter?
MADJE: If Papa had come downstairs and discovered his virgin daughter in flagrante! . . .
ASCH: I would never have made it to the huppah alive.
MADJE: It's interesting to hear your words the night you seduced me . . . in the mouth of a prostitute.

ASCH: I feel like a prostitute every time I have to pander to Mr. Peretz to get a reading in his salon.

MADJE: This play will cause a sensation tomorrow night! All the writers will be green with envy.

ASCH: Don't bring down the evil eye! Mr. Peretz could hate it.

MADJE: Oh, Mr. Peretz is a lovely man . . . but he's so nineteenth century.

Acchh! Warsaw is a provincial little town! This play will be done all over the world: Moscow, Berlin, Paris— wait, wait!—I know who would be perfect for the father! Rudolph Schildkraut!

ASCH: Who?

MADJE: Rudolph Schildkraut is a sensation in Berlin right now with his *Merchant of Venice*. I'll ask Papa for money to send you. We must get this play to him!

ASCH: It's my first play!

MADJE: Our play will catch fire in Berlin! All the German intelligentsia can talk about right now is Dr. Freud! It's the twentieth century! We are all attracted to both sexes. I promise I'll understand if you get attracted to a man—

ASCH: —Huh.

MADJE: But I'll kill you if it's another woman.

ASCH: I promise you I'll understand if you get attracted to a woman—as long as I can watch.

MADJE: My God, I am now married to a *playwright*! You're my warrior! My suffragette!

ASCH *(Hopefully)*: Your lesbian?

MADJE: "Teach me. Take me. I want to taste you."

(Madje dives beneath the covers.)

1906: A Salon at the Peretz Home

ASCH: First of all I want to say what a great honor it is to have this opportunity . . . to be—to be under Mr. Peretz's roof, to be standing here in front of all of these writers whose work has been such an inspiration . . .

(Asch wipes the sweat from his brow; passes out the scripts. Peretz looks at his:)

PERETZ *(Reading)*: THE GOD OF VENGEANCE!

NAKHMEN: It's a one-hundred-and-thirty-page three-act play. What a prodigy! Does anyone mind if Lemml sits in? He's my third cousin from Łódź.

LEMML: Well, a little shtetl outside Balut actually . . .

NAKHMEN: He's a tailor from Balut—he's never seen a play!

PERETZ *(Eager to welcome a working man)*: Lemml! Take a seat, take a seat!

(Peretz goes to shake Lemml's hand. Lemml nervously wipes his hands on his jacket before he will touch Peretz.)

LEMML: Sir. It's a real honor, sir.

PERETZ: Welcome.

(Nakhmen quickly thumbs through the script.)

NAKHMEN: Oy. Another play set in a brothel.

PERETZ: Why are so many men writing brothel stories?

NAKHMEN *(In a low voice to Peretz)*: Research.

(The men laugh.)

ASCH: Mr. Peretz would you read Yekel?

NAKHMEN (*Reading the title page*): You want Mr. Peretz to play the owner of a brothel?

ASCH: I want him to play the protagonist. He has the most lines.

PERETZ: Ahh! I will do my humble best.

ASCH: Lazar you read Rifkele. The daughter. She's seventeen. She's pure. And very beautiful. Isaac, her mother, Sarah. Smart. Ambitious. An ex-prostitute.

(*The men raise their eyebrows.*)

Nakhmen, you read Manke the prostitute. She's in her twenties: the beauty of Yekel's stable. Don't use your chest voice.

(*Nakhmen takes the script. The two men blink at each other.*)

I'll read stage directions. "As the curtain rises, we find ourselves in Yekel's cozy home over the basement where his brothel is located. There he lives with his virgin daughter and his wife . . ."

A BLINK IN TIME

IN THE MIDST OF ACT ONE

PERETZ (*As Yekel*): Woman: I am not going to warn you again. When I took you from my whorehouse I told you: keep my home apart from my whores! I'd better not catch Rifkele in Manke's company again!

(*A little thrill in the room because Peretz has said the word whorehouse and whore.*)

Up here lives my virgin daughter, worthy of marrying the best of men. Like the kosher from the traif! Keep the two worlds apart!

A BLINK IN TIME

Act Two: The First Rain Scene

ASCH (*Reading stage directions*): Manke enters, nuzzling Rifkele. Washed in the rain, their soaked nightgowns drip water on the floor . . .

NAKHMEN (*As Manke*): Are you shivering, Rifkele? Warm yourself—rub up against me, that feels—

ASCH (*Sotto voce to Nakhmen*): Higher voice, please . . .

NAKHMEN (*As Manke*): Rest your face against my—

(*Asch steals a glance at an impassive Peretz. Nakhmen stops.*)

Wait. Wait. Am I still a woman here? Saying this to another woman? I am not reading this garbage.

(*He tosses the script down. Asch picks up the discarded script and gives it to Lemml.*)

ASCH: Read Manke's lines, starting with "Rest your face against my breasts—"

LEMML: You want me to say the word "breasts" in this living room?

ASCH: Read, damn it!

LEMML (*As Manke*): Rest your face against, against my . . . breasts (*Takes a breath, plunges on*) Yes, oh yes . . . And embrace me with your body.

(*A small involuntary shiver from Lemml: Ooooh. He gets stronger:*)

16

I laid bare your breasts and I washed them in the rain.
You smell like grass in the meadows ... Do you want me
to ... Rifkele, do you want us to?
ASCH: Rifkele ...

(Lazar refuses to read.)

NAKHMEN: None of us are reading this garbage!

(The three men toss their scripts to the floor.)

PERETZ: Well, perhaps we should call it a—
ASCH *(To Lemml)*: You have to read both women. Manke and
Rifkele. Please.
LEMML *(As Rifkele)*: I ... I have never done one woman, much
less two, Mr. Asch!
ASCH: Okay. You read Rifkele. I'll be Manke. *(As Manke)* You
smell like grass in the meadows ... Do you want me to ...
Rifkele, do you want us to?
LEMML *(As Rifkele)*: Yes. Yes. *(He sees the next line; closes his eyes,
takes a deep breath)* Teach me. Take me. I want to taste you.
ASCH *(As Manke)*: I can't breathe.

(The men in the salon can't either.)

A BLINK IN TIME

THE LAST MOMENTS OF THE PLAY

PERETZ *(As Yekel)*: Rifkele: You ran away with Manke last
night. Don't tell me where she took you. Daughter, just tell
me: Are you still a virgin? Let me see into your eyes! Right
into your eyes!
LEMML *(As Rifkele)*: I ... don't know.

PERETZ (*As Yekel*): What do you mean—you don't know! Are
you still a—

LEMML (*As Rifkele*): Oh, but it's all right for you to do? I know
who you are and what you do!

PERETZ (*As Yekel*): I'll tell you what you know. You know
what this Torah cost? It cost all of the whores downstairs
on their backs and their knees for a year! And for what?
Look at Me! God wants me to fail as a father? As a husband? Well there's one thing I know how to do—MAKE
MONEY. You are both paying me back! On your backs.
On your knees.

Down into the whorehouse with you!! And take the
Holy Scroll with you! I don't need it anymore!

ASCH (*Reading stage directions*): Yekel hurls down the Torah.
End of play.

LEMML (*Crying*): This is Theater?!! Oh. Oh, Mr. Asch. It is
wonderful.

NAKHMEN: Are you crying? Asch has desecrated the Torah!

ASCH: My character Yekel does—I do not!—

LEMML: But it's not a real Torah, right, Mr. Asch? / It's a make-
believe Torah—

NAKHMEN: Grandmother Rochel's daughter's son: You are
way out of your depths here. I brought you here as a favor
to your mother.

LEMML: It was a very big favor, cousin.

NAKHMEN: "Do you want me to, Rifkele, do you want us to?
Yes, yes . . ."

(*Nakhmen and the others burst into laughter.*)

ASCH: How can you let Nakhmen laugh at me!

PERETZ: We need to have a civil discourse no matter what the
young men in my living room do. (*Beat*) Or write.

ASCH: My soul is in these pages!

PERETZ: Asch. Asch. Who is your audience?

ASCH: I want to write for everyone.

LEMML (*To himself*): Yes—

ASCH: —You told me we need plays in Yiddish which are universal.

PERETZ: Plays that represent our people as valiant, heroic—

ASCH: —Why must every Jew onstage be a paragon?!!

NAKHMEN: You are representing our people as prostitutes and pimps!

ASCH: Some of our people are!

PERETZ: You are pouring petrol on the flames of anti-Semitism. This is not the time.

ASCH: When! When will be the right time?

PERETZ: For God's sake, Asch—write what you know, young man! How many whorehouses have you worked in?

(*Mrs. Peretz carries a vial of medicine and a glass of water across the room to Mr. Peretz. The men stand.*)

Ah yes. It's time for my medicine. Thank you, my dear.

MRS. PERETZ (*Looking icily at Asch*): And did you have a nice reading, Mr. Asch?

ASCH: Yes, ma'am.

MRS. PERETZ: I loved your last short story: "A Shtetl." So *lyrical*. There seems to be . . . much excitement in the house. Excitement is not the best thing for Mr. Peretz's digestion.

ASCH: We . . . won't keep him much longer.

MRS. PERETZ: I think I've had enough excitement myself. Excuse me.

(*She closes the door behind her.*)

ASCH: Mr. Peretz—it is because of you that we are creating a Yiddish renaissance—

PERETZ: Come, come—Yiddish is our mother tongue. The language of our myths, our songs . . .

ASCH: Our streets. Our gutters. Our desire.

LEMML: Yes . . .

PERETZ: At the end of every day I come home from work, kiss my wife and go into this study. And four nights of the week I try to write something for the Jewish people. It may get no further than this living room but it's for us.

ASCH: I am not happy to produce one slim volume of poetry every two or three years that gets read in your living room. I am not ashamed because I want our stories to be on every stage in every language.

PERETZ: You cannot translate . . . this hateful play. If you must throw stones, throw them outside the tent.

NAKHMEN: Oy veh iz mir. This is a play written by a Jew who hates Jews!

ASCH: Do you know what a minyan is? It's ten Jews in a circle accusing each other of anti-Semitism.

PERETZ: Sholem! You will be torn limb from limb if the public sees this play. Listen to me: about your manuscript? —BURN IT.

ASCH: Mr. Lemml, may I buy you a drink? I'm taking my stones outside the tent with me. I've always wanted to see Berlin.

(*We suddenly find ourselves in a Berlin cabaret, early twentieth century. The atmosphere is saturated with erotic tension. The troupe dances with their suitcases, displaying every vice to be enjoyed by a tourist on the prowl. Even the musicians get into the act.*)

1908, BERLIN: A CABARET

"SUITCASE IN BERLIN"

Halina sings "Suitcase in Berlin":

HALINA:

Wunderschön ist's in Paris auf der Rue Madeleine.	*It's wonderful in Paris on the Rue Madeleine.*

Schön ist es im Mai in Rom durch die Stadt zu gehen. Oder eine Sommernacht still beim Wein in Wien. Doch ich häng wenn ihr auch lacht,	*It's beautiful during May in Rome to stroll through the city. Or during a summer night to quietly drink wine in Vienna. But I'd rather hang out even if you laugh,*

(The cast sings:)

CAST:

    Heut' noch an Berlin.   *Today in Berlin.*

(Otto sings:)

OTTO:

Ich hab' noch einen Koffer in Berlin. Deswegen muss ich nächstens wieder hin. Die Seligkeiten vergangener Zeiten Sind alle noch in meinem kleinen Koffer drin.	*I still have a suitcase in Berlin. That's why I have to go there soon. The joys of days gone by* *Are still in my little suitcase.*

(Avram and Otto sing:)

AVRAM AND OTTO:

Ich hab' noch einen Koffer in Berlin. Der bleibt auch dort, und das hat seinen Sinn.	*I still have a suitcase in Berlin. It stays there, and that makes sense.*

(Halina, Avram and Otto sing:)

HALINA, AVRAM AND OTTO:

Auf diese Weise	*In this way*

(Chana sings:)

CHANA:

Lohnt sich die Reise	*It's worth a trip*

(The cast sings:)

CAST:

Denn wenn ich Sehnsucht hab' dann	*So whenever I have a longing*
Fahr' ich wieder hin.	*Then I can go back again.*

(Violin/viola duet.)

Auf diese Weise lohnt sich die Reise	*In this way it's worth a trip*
Denn wenn ich Sehnsucht hab' dann	*So whenever I have a longing*
Fahr' ich wieder hin.	*Then I can go back again.*

1908, BERLIN: THE DEUTSCHES THEATRE
ELSA HEIMES AND FREIDA NIEMANN

IN GERMAN:

FREIDA: And you must be Fräulein Elsa!

ELSA: I cannot believe I get to be in a play with the legendary Freida Niemann!

FREIDA: Please, please—the legend is flesh and blood, I assure you. —Have you read the script?

ELSA: Oh yes, several times. It's very daring, I think.

FREIDA: Oh good. You can explain it all to me.

ELSA: You haven't read it?

FREIDA: Oh, no. I like to find the role through intuition.

Of course, when Rudolph came to me: "Freida, we have a role, this young boy must have been thinking of you when he wrote it . . ."

And I positively peppered him with questions: How do these women live? How do they dress? What do they do in bed and how do they do it?

ELSA: You mean prostitutes?

FREIDA: Oh good God, no! We all know what prostitutes do!

ELSA: Oh—so you asked him about . . . about . . . lesbians?

FREIDA: You'd better learn how to say the word out loud, my girl. Four weeks from today we will be kissing center stage. (By the way, my left profile is my good profile.) I mean, I haven't read the play yet, but I assume I will be the butch, and you are the feminine little thing.

But on one thing I am completely lost at sea: How do I play a Jew?

(Elsa blinks at Freida.)

Or is the proper word Jewess?

ELSA: Mrs. Freida, I am Jewish.

FREIDA: That is very brave of you.

ELSA: Very, very secular, very . . .

FREIDA: I consider us, first and foremost, German.

(Lemml enters.)

LEMML: Excuse me, Mrs. Excuse me, Miss. Mr. Schildkraut asking me to asking you—what for you may I geht?

FREIDA: Isn't he just adorable! What is your name, kind sir?

LEMML: Lemml my name is. I—happiness—have serve you—

ELSA: —How long have you been in Berlin, Herr Lemml?

LEMML: This is the first week I come Berlin. / This is the first week I come Germany!

FREIDA: Herr Lemml, please speak Yiddish, if you like. I must sound like one of the hordes overrunning—like—well, a native, if you will.

(Lemml sighs from relief.)

THEY LAUNCH INTO YIDDISH:

LEMML: Thank you, Mrs.! I cannot believe I get this opportunity—a job in the theater!

Assistant to the stage manager!—I could never imagine such a thing in Balut. And this play—this play! I was working as a tailor in a little shop but one night my cousin said I could come with him to Mr. Peretz's house—and I got to hear the play of the genius Sholem Asch!

FREIDA: Oh, a genius? A Yiddish genius—a polack genius!—

LEMML *(Softly)*: They got genius outside of Germany, too. This play will be done all over the world.

(The troupe has wandered in for the first rehearsal.)

RUDOLPH SCHILDKRAUT MAKES AN ENTRANCE

Asch steps to the stage behind Rudolph Schildkraut.

IN GERMAN:

SCHILDKRAUT: Lemml! Where are you?

LEMML: I here am, Mr. Schildkraut.

(The troupe laughs.)

24

SCHILDKRAUT: Call the company to the stage!

LEMML: To the stage please come!

(Schildkraut nods to Freida, then kisses Elsa's hand.
When Schildkraut has an audience:)

SCHILDKRAUT: Good morning, good morning! Today we gather in this august building where we last rehearsed *The Merchant of Venice!*—to peddle a different pound of flesh! As you know, a few short months ago, I was "stalked" by a young gentleman. As I was sipping my mélange in the Café Kranzler, a Polish countryman approached me with such fresh energy and sincerity—traits that have almost perished in our cosmopolitan Berlin! That very night I went home with his script and I woke up with a fever to produce *The God of Vengeance.* To play this outcast rejected by pious Jews roaring at his maker! Ladies, gentlemen, I give you our playwright of this brilliant little play: Mr. Sholem Asch.

ASCH: Thank you, thank you. I don't want to terrify you—but this is my first play.

This past fall I sat down at my desk in Warsaw and I asked myself: How do we as artists question our sins in front of a greater audience? How do we as Jews show ourselves as flawed and complex human beings? Never did I dream that this great artist would choose to inhabit a man on the edge of our society, wrestling with his sins and his God.

I've written only poetry and short stories, alone at my desk. And I never realized that when one writes a play, one is no longer alone—

FREIDA: Oy.

SCHILDKRAUT: Let's begin!

A BLINK IN TIME

1908, Berlin: Opening Night, the Last Moments of the Play

Asch stands beside Lemml near the curtain backstage.

YEKEL: Daughter, just tell me! Are you still a virgin? Let me see right into your eyes!! Right into your eyes!!

RIFKELE: I . . . don't know.

YEKEL: What do you mean—you don't know! Are you still—

RIFKELE: Oh, but it's all right for you to do? I know who you are and what you do!

YEKEL: I'll tell you what you know. You know what this Torah cost? It cost all of the whores downstairs on their backs and their knees for a year! And for what? Look at me. God wants me to fail as a father? As a husband? Well there's one thing I know how to do—MAKE MONEY. You are both paying me back! On your backs. On your knees.

(Sarah tries to grab her daughter away, but Yekel strikes his wife. As his wife cries, he drags his daughter by the hair. Rifkele cries.)

Down into the whorehouse with you!

(Rifkele weeps . . . it is a hideous sound.)

SARAH: Help, he's going crazy!

(She tries to pull Rifkele away from Yekel, who "hits" her away.)

YEKEL: Down into the whorehouse with you! And take the Holy Scroll with you! I don't need it anymore!

(Yekel raises the Scroll but does not throw the Torah. The lights dim as a curtain falls. Riotous applause.)

A BLINK IN TIME

1911, St. Petersburg

SARAH: Help, he's going crazy!
YEKEL: And take the Holy Scroll with you! I don't need it anymore!

A BLINK IN TIME

1914, Constantinople

SARAH: Help, he's going crazy!
YEKEL: And take the Holy Scroll with you! I don't need it anymore!

A BLINK IN TIME

1918, Bratislava

SARAH: Help, he's going crazy!
YEKEL: And take the Holy Scroll with you! I don't need it anymore!

(The entire troupe is lined up in the Great Hall at Ellis Island.)

1920, Ellis Island: An Impossibly Long Line

a blink in time

Lemml is toward the end of the line.

ASCH: Lemml! Lemml! / Over here! Lemml!

LEMML: Mr. Asch! Mr. Asch! Mr. Asch!

ASCH: I can't wait to stand beside you next week when you raise the curtain on *The God of Vengeance* at the Bowery Theatre. It hasn't been the same. The troupe can't wait to meet you!

LEMML: Mr. Asch: How did you do such a thing? Back there: the weeping, the pleading. —They are sending so many people back—but I got in!

ASCH: There were a few strings we could pull . . .

LEMML: Of course! Because you are Sholem Asch!

Nobody in Balut believed you sent for me when I came to say good-bye!

ASCH: You were my first advocate.

LEMML: My life! It is changed!

ASCH: I want to see your face when you see it:

Sholem Asch Shows Lemml America

Asch shows Lemml the harbor of New York, the shore of Manhattan.

ASCH: Welcome to America!

LEMML: America! I here am!

> (*A song. Subtitles translate the song's lyrics from Yiddish into English. The troupe has just gotten through the hazing process of Ellis Island. Hopeful, scared, they line up as Hasidim and sing. They*

are dressed in their Saturday best from the Old Country. As they sing, and celebrate their entry into America, they slowly strip their shtetl clothes. One by one, they shed their peyes. One older Hasid reacts with a growing terror as he finds himself in the midst of nattily dressed immigrants. By the end of the song, they have removed his peyes, given him a top hat—together, the now Americanized chorus does a kick-line, and the former older Hasid can outkick them all.)

"VOT KEN YOU MAKH IN AMERICA?"

Mendel sings "Vot Ken You Makh in America?":

MENDEL:

> Keyn Amerike tzu kumen, hob ikh keyn mi geshport,
> kh'hob gedenkt a rov tzu vern un farlosn zikh a bord.
> Kh'hob gehat tzvey sheyne peyes, vi yeder frumer yid
> Tzum sof onshtot a bord hob ikh di peyes oykhet nit.

(Avram sings:)

AVRAM:

> Vet ir mir fregn: S'taytsh? Vi ken dos zayn?

(Chana sings:)

CHANA:

> Der terets derfun iz, libe fraynt mayn':

(Mendel sings:)

MENDEL:

> Vot ken you makh? Es iz Amerike!

(Otto sings:)

OTTO:

Do in land do pitzt men zikh azoy.

(*The cast sings:*)

CAST:

Vot ken you makh? Es iz Amerike!

(*Avram sings:*)

AVRAM:

Afile der yid hot dem ponim fin a goy.

(*Halina sings:*)

HALINA:

Az fun peyes do zet men bay keynem nisht keyn shpor,
Do trogn zikh di peyelech ale meydlekh gor.'

(*Otto, Vera and Lemml sing:*)

OTTO, VERA AND LEMML:

Vot ken you makh? Es iz Amerike,

(*Halina, Avram, Mendel and Chana sing:*)

HALINA, AVRAM, MENDEL AND CHANA:

S'iz Amerike, un vot ken you makh?

(*The cast sings:*)

CAST:

What can you makh dis is America!
Iz America, un vot ken you makh?

THE CAST SINGS THE SONG IN ENGLISH:

CAST:
> To come to America, I took great trouble.
> I thought I'd become a rabbi and grow myself a beard.
> I had two beautiful peyes, like every religious Jew.
> But in the end, I had no beard and my peyes were gone.
>
> Oh, you ask me how can this be?
> The answer is, my dear friend:
> What can you do? It's America!
> That's how people look here!
> What can you do? It's America!
> Even a Jew looks like a goy!
>
> You don't see any trace of peyes,
> Here, it's only the girls who wear them!
>
> What can you do? It's America!
> It's America, so what can you do?

1921, New York City: The Bowery Theatre

SARAH: Gvald! Er iz meshige gevorn!

YEKEL: Dos seyfer-toyre nemt aykh mit, ikh darf es shoyn nisht mer!

(The sound of thunderous applause. Curtain call.)

A BLINK IN TIME

1922, NEW YORK CITY: REHEARSAL FOR
THE ENGLISH TRANSFER

Dorothee and Reina are in the midst of a fight.

FAST AND IN YIDDISH:

DOROTHEE: English! Speak English! —Every time we are alone
together, you persist in speaking Yiddish! My God, Reina,
we are supposed to open this show in English next week!
REINA: I don't need your permission to speak Yiddish when we
are in private!
DOROTHEE: Reina! We are the first generation that gets the
chance our parents never got. To tell our stories. On American
stages. We are moving uptown to the Village and
I want you to go with me! Please speak English with me!

FROM HERE ON THEY SPEAK IN ENGLISH:

REINA: Ruth. You can call me Reina at home. Sit. Beside me.
Let's just run lines.
DOROTHEE: From Sarah's lines: "Brush your hair, get dressed.
The minyan's on its way."

*(Reina reaches for Dorothee's hands. Reina speaks English with a
thick Lithuanian accent:)*

REINA: I'll call Manke to come brush mein hor. I love it when
she brushes mein hor. Mein hor—
DOROTHEE: —Hair—

REINA: Mein chhh-hair!—gets so smooth.

(Reina stops. They know it is useless.)

IN YIDDISH:

REINA: Mr. Schildkraut won't replace me.
DOROTHEE: We've got a week to learn the English translation.
REINA: And from now on . . . only English between us? Deine?
I do not know who this Dorothee is.

IN ENGLISH:

DOROTHEE: It's my name now. Dorothee is the same woman
you love as Deine.

(Schildkraut enters with Lemml.)

SCHILDKRAUT: Ladies? Will you pardon my intrusion? I would
like to speak to Miss Ruth.

(Dorothee stands.)

DOROTHEE: I'll go.
REINA: She stay.

*(Schildkraut lumbers to a bench and sits. Lemml stands. He shares
a look with Dorothee.)*

SCHILDKRAUT: Oy yoy yoy. A long day. Miss Ruth: It's no
good. I talk the way I talk. Miss Dorothee talks better.
But when people hear Rifkele they got to hear a pure girl
onstage. No shtetl, no girl off the boat. They got to see

their own American daughter. We have to let you go. You will be a beauty for our people on the Yiddish stage for decades to come. Zay moykhl. (*I'm sorry.*)

REINA: In English. You tell me leave in English.

SCHILDKRAUT: I am sorry.

DOROTHEE: Mr. Schildkraut? Ruth and I can rehearse all night until—

REINA: You and Lemml already run lines with me. Nothing help. Unless you want to quit with me, Deine, no? I thought not. Go please, Mr. Schildkraut.

(*The two women watch Schildkraut leave with thespian dignity.*)

DOROTHEE: Reina—

REINA: Gay avek. Jetz.
Lemml blayb.

Go Away. Now. Lemml Stay.

DOROTHEE: I'll see you at home.

(*Dorothee leaves. Lemml speaks softly in Yiddish:*)

LEMML: I am so sorry, Miss Reina.

REINA: When did you know?

LEMML: Two days ago. I was told to say nothing.

REINA: My role—

LEMML: They have already recast Rifkele.

REINA: This will be the only role in my lifetime where I could tell someone I love that I love her onstage.

LEMML: I will come see you on the Yiddish stage and throw flowers.

REINA: It may be quite some time before I find a job again. So throw food. Thank you, Lemml.

LEMML: Mr. Schildkraut says I gotta have an American name for the Greenwich Village too. It's Lou. Lou.

(*Reina kisses Lemml's cheek.*)

REINA (*In English*): Good-bye, Lou.

(*Reina leaves. Lemml finds his broom, and sweeps the rehearsal room.*)

Introducing Virginia McFadden

Esther, a middle-aged actress, holding her script, but off-book, paces out the blocking she knows by heart in rehearsal. She's fast.

Dorothee, Rudolph, and Lemml rehearse. Morris Carnovsky watches.

IN ENGLISH:

LEMML: "A bridegroom? Who is he, Mama?"

VIRGINIA: "A bridegroom? Who is he, Mama?"

ESTHER: "A darling boy, a treasure from a wonderful family. And handsome like a rabbi!"

(*Beat. Esther breaks character. To Virginia:*)

Okay, this is where you speak your line.

VIRGINIA: Do I say it from here?

ESTHER: Rudolph! Zog der shikse vu ahin tsu geyn!

CARNOVSKY: She's asking where the beautiful young lady might go. Morris Carnovsky ... I play Shloyme, one of the pimps.

SCHILDKRAUT: Miss McFadden. Now you go to Dorothee. As if you was gonna hug your fiancé before you was married. —Yes! Miss McFadden! Perfect! Now! You say!

VIRGINIA: Where are we going to live, Mama?

ESTHER: —Is it break time, yet? Ich volt azihk farkovfn far a papiros.

CARNOVSKY: She's saying she'd sell herself for a cigarette.

SCHILDKRAUT: Morris Carnovsky?! You are not in this scene!

CARNOVSKY: I'm here to help translate . . .

SCHILDKRAUT: Sha! Where was we?

DOROTHEE: She's hugging me like her fiancé—

SCHILDKRAUT: —Sha! Sha! Miss McFadden. Now you are gonna kiss Dorothee the way you gonna kiss your husband on your wedding night . . .

CARNOVSKY: Lucky young man!

DOROTHEE: Are you all right with this?

VIRGINIA (Scared): Yes.

(Carnovsky and Schildkraut lean in. Dorothee kisses Virginia, gently. Virginia takes a breath and kisses Dorothee back with a bit more conviction.)

SCHILDKRAUT: Wunderbar!   CARNOVSKY: Nice work, nice
                                                work!

ESTHER (Who just wants her cigarette break): Oy!

SCHILDKRAUT: So you want to just lay yourself against her . . . it is now the morning after and you are two happy cats who lecken the kreme . . .

VIRGINIA: Excuse me, Mr. Schildkraut, but could you tell me in English?

SCHILDKRAUT: I am speaking in the English!

DOROTHEE: Place my hand where you feel comfortable.

(Virginia does so. The two settle in to each other . . .)

SCHILDKRAUT: Can you move your hands up to her bristen more, Dorothee?

DOROTHEE: —I am not a happy cat . . .

LEMML: —I don't got nothin' like that in my pages, Mr. Schild-kraut.

SCHILDKRAUT: Sut katsen.

LEMML: Ten minutes, ladies, gentlemen.

DOROTHEE: Thank you, Lemml.

VIRGINIA: Thank you, Lemml.

LEMML: Just call me Lou. —And may I say, Miss McFadden, I have been wid this show from the first show, and I seen all the shows of this show . . . You are gonna be magnificent!
(*Calling out*) Ten minutes!

(*He leaves. A moment.*)

DOROTHEE: I know this must be hard to step in like this, but you are doing a great job.

VIRGINIA: I don't mean to terrify you, but . . . this is my first show.

DOROTHEE (*Terrified*): That is brave. I mean—this show!

VIRGINIA: I'm hoping it shocks my parents. When can I meet the playwright?

DOROTHEE: Sholem Asch has practically become a recluse on Staten Island! He works very hard on his novels. I love his work. Sholem Asch shows women as flesh and blood! How hard it is—it was—
. . . Mr. Schildkraut compares the rain scene in Act Two to the balcony scene in *Romeo and Juliet*. The scene in the rain for me is . . . is just so . . . I'm having a hard time with English today.

VIRGINIA: It's lesbian, right?

DOROTHEE: What?

VIRGINIA: Did I misread the play? I thought we were lesbians.

DOROTHEE: I—I—

VIRGINIA: Did I say something wrong?

DOROTHEE: I like to think all the layers of love—sister, mother, daughter—

VIRGINIA: —Should we practice kissing?

DOROTHEE: What?

VIRGINIA: I mean, before we have to do it in front of every-one—should we try it by ourselves?

DOROTHEE: I thought you did a great job of it before the break.

VIRGINIA: I just thought. Sorry. You certainly do not need any practice, I must say.

DOROTHEE (*Starting to sweat*): Why don't we first just try it on the cheek in rehearsal . . . and then, and then we can, we can—

VIRGINIA: Yes. Perhaps we should save the lips for opening night.

DOROTHEE: Do you have any training? In acting I mean?

VIRGINIA: My parents would never have let me. And at Smith there was no theater really—

DOROTHEE: Oh. Smith. As in College?

VIRGINIA: Yes. I've been around lots of girls, so that should help . . . in *this* play.

DOROTHEE: What will shock your parents the most: that you are playing in a Jewish company? That you are playing a Jewish girl? Or that you are playing a girl in love with a prostitute?

VIRGINIA: I hope all of it! (*She laughs*)

A BLINK IN TIME

Opening Night at the Provincetown Playhouse: In the Wings

We watch Virginia and Lemml offstage and the performance onstage. Offstage:

LEMML: It's a wonderful job you are doing, Miss Virginia.

VIRGINIA: I can't stop my body from shaking.

LEMML: It's only your first time onstage. The fright . . .

VIRGINIA: Whenever I see Dorothee . . . I feel her onstage so much I get scared I will go up on my lines.

LEMML: You have to feel what Rifkele feels. Yes? This is what happens to actors. It's a good thing.

VIRGINIA: It's hard to breathe.

LEMML: I know nothing about the Christian Church. You was brought up in the Church?

VIRGINIA: Yes.

LEMML: Maybe how your Rifkele feels for Manke is a sin in your Church. In this play, how you feel for her and she for you—to me—after the Messiah comes. No hate. No beating. No sin.

A BLINK IN TIME

The Performance

Onstage:

SARAH: Rifkele, Rifkele, I need your help. Your papa and the rabbi will be here soon with the Torah Scroll.

(Offstage:)

LEMML: Ssssh. Breathe deep. Just look at Miss Dorothee while you shake. Your cue, it is coming . . .

(Onstage:)

SARAH: Rifkele, Rivekele. They'll be here any minute.

LEMML *(Offstage)*: Now. Geht.

(*Virginia goes onstage as Rifkele. Dorothee appears for her cue. Together Dorothee and Lemml watch.*
  Onstage:)

RIFKELE: I'll call Manke to come up and brush my hair. I love it when she brushes my hair. My hair gets so smooth. (*Tapping on the floor*) —Manke! Manke!
SARAH: Rifkele! Don't! Papa's gonna break our necks!

(*Sarah goes into another room. We hear her call Rifkele from offstage:*)

I told you to stop seeing that girl! You got nothing in common! The guests will be here any moment ... We're arranging a bridegroom for you.
RIFKELE: A bridegroom? Who is he, Mama?
SARAH: A wonderful boy, a treasure from a wonderful family. Handsome like a rabbi.

(*Dorothee takes a deep, nervous breath and, as Manke, enters onstage.*
  Sarah is still in the other room, offstage.
  Rifkele goes to Manke. The room starts growing dark.)

RIFKELE (*Off, to her mother*): Where will we live, Mama?

(*Manke and Rifkele look at each other. Manke kisses Rifkele ardently. Rifkele falls into Manke's arms. She strokes Manke's cheek.*)

SARAH: In your bedroom right under your papa's roof! There beneath the Holy Scroll your papa bought, you will do your wifely duty!
RIFKELE: Will he love me, Mama?
SARAH: Very much, my dearest daughter. Every night.

(*Lemml and Esther watch the climax of Act One with bated breath.*)

The Curtain Falls

Onstage: Virginia breaks from Dorothee's hold and faces her. That was not in the script. Virginia, shaking, throws herself on Dorothee, nuzzling her neck.

Offstage: Lemml waits with open arms for Virginia as she exits. She runs into his embrace. Dorothee walks into the wings behind her.

LEMML: Beautiful.

(Virginia starts to cry.)

VIRGINIA: I don't ever want to stop acting. Ever.

Full Company Meeting:
The Provincetown Playhouse

IN ENGLISH:

The troupe is assembled. Harry Weinberger sits, beaming. Lemml holds a stack of scripts.

SCHILDKRAUT: Ladies, gentleman, I give you our producer at the Greenwich Theatre: Mr. Harry Weinberger!

(The troupe applauds.)

HARRY: Of all the places in New York I have called home—the courtroom, the picket line, the labor unions—the best home for me has been standing in the back of the orchestra at the Provincetown Players.

I got in on the ground floor as producer of a little play by a wild Irishman, name of Eugene O'Neill—*The Hairy Ape?* So I have recently found a new home on Broadway.

And it got me thinking: What if a play came my way written by a fellow Jew that told our stories?

So I'm here to announce: Two weeks from today *The God of Vengeance*, starring Rudolph Schildkraut, opens at The Apollo Theatre on Broadway!

(Dorothee runs in, script clenched in hand.)

DOROTHEE: I am *not* acting in this garbage. They've cut the rain scene.

(Dorothee throws the script on the floor. Schildkraut picks it up and looks at the title page.)

SCHILDKRAUT: Did I not say to you to keep the new scripts to yourself?

HARRY: Miss Nelson, I was about to ask you for a coffee after—

(The troupe starts to grab and pass around the new scripts.)

DOROTHEE: Did Mr. Asch censor his own play?

HARRY: Every day downtown we are sold out. Every day another stack of hate mail arrives. And I read every single letter that comes in: "Jews. Polacks! Take your filth back to your own country. Dirty kikes. You pollute our stage." That's what we're up against.

DOROTHEE: Did the playwright agree to cuts in the most beautiful love scene he will ever write?

SCHILDKRAUT: We told him and he signed the contract with the same hand that cashed the check.

HARRY: For now, we have to strengthen the moral argument for audiences on Broadway.

VIRGINIA: Dorothee—they cut our rain scene?

DOROTHEE: My Manke is no longer a woman in love. She is an evil procuress lusting after a little girl to peddle her ass. Now instead of us falling in love in this obscenity of a world, instead of me trying to rescue you—the new script has me entrapping you into a life of white slavery! I've been promoted to Head Pimp!

HARRY: Miss Nelson, I don't want to hurt your feelings, but this production cannot be seen to celebrate two women in love! After we open we can restore—

SCHILDKRAUT: Miss Dorothee—I could make my Broadway debut in many many shows. Shakespeare. Chekhov. George Bernard Shaw. I chose a new play by a living Yiddish writer.

LEMML: We are potchkying wid' a masterpiece. God forbid the goyim think ladies who work the street are human beings! God forbid the goyim think that Jewish ladies love each other as human beings! A shanda fur die goy! We could let the original script speak for us.

ESTHER: Look, here's what's gonna happen. Mr. and Mrs. Smith get on the train from Connecticut. They bring Junior and their daughter to the matinee. And what Mr. Weinberger don't want to see is a red-faced Mr. Smith pulling Junior out of his orchestra seats and marching the Smith family up the aisles. Because Junior was getting a little too excited and they're gonna spend the train ride explaining to their daughter why these two girls are kissing—let's just say the farshtinkeneh word: among the intelligentsia lesbians sell tickets. Uptown, for Mr. and Mrs. Smith, prostitutes in a brothel is all the excitement they can take.

LEMML: Mr. Weinberger, did you know, every night during the rain scene, the entire troupe lines up in the wings to watch.

ESTHER: It's true.

SCHILDKRAUT: I watch from stage left.

CARNOVSKY: Stage right in the wings.

LEMML: In Berlin. In Moscow. In the Village. Every night. The entire troupe.

DOROTHEE: I—I've sacrificed a lot to play this one flesh-and-blood woman.

HARRY: If anyone here can't accommodate the changes to the script, now would be a good time to let us know . . .

(Silence. Dorothee stands still. Lemml goes to her and puts his arm around her shoulder. Beat. Another time, another light.)

"AIN'T WE GOT FUN"

We watch the actors perform an American hit song from 1923 Broadway: "Ain't We Got Fun." The cast sings:

CAST:
> Every morning, every evening
> Ain't we got fun?
> Not much money, oh, but, honey
> Ain't we got fun?
>
> There's nothing surer
> The rich get rich and the poor get laid off
> In the meantime, in between time . . .

1923: A Doctor, a Diagnosis

IN ENGLISH:

MADJE: He has not slept for weeks. Every evening he leaves our bed. Every morning I find him awake in his study.

DR. HORNIG: Was there anything about the last few months that was abnormal in your routine, Mr. Asch?

IN YIDDISH:

MADJE: Tell her about Kiev. Tell her about Vilna.

IN ENGLISH:

ASCH: I have just returned from a trip to Europe . . .
MADJE: He was the head of a delegation for the American Jewish Joint Committee. A fact-finding trip to Europe.
HORNIG: Ah! The Old Country.
MADJE: He was investigating pogroms. Vilna, Kiev.
HORNIG: Oh.
ASCH: The Old Country.
MADJE: He will not talk to me about what he saw. He has not been himself since his return.
HORNIG: How would he describe not being himself?

IN YIDDISH:

MADJE: She wants to know how you feel.
ASCH: I'm unable to sleep. Lack of concentration. Lack of appetite, lack of enjoyment.

IN ENGLISH:

MADJE: A great deal of lack . . . He doesn't leave the house. He is about to have his Broadway debut, and he hasn't gone to a single rehearsal! Every day the stage manager calls, "Where is your husband, Mrs. Asch?"
HORNIG: Here's a prescription of Seconal. You are exhibiting nervous exhaustion—

MADJE: What can we do?

HORNIG: Complete bed rest is often quite successful with women and writers.

For men, however, going West is better suited to the restoration of masculine vitality and energy. Cattle roping, treks in the Rockies, buffalo hunting if there are any buffalo to be found.

IN YIDDISH:

MADJE: She gives you a choice of being strapped to your bed or—buffalo hunting.

ASCH (Angry): Ask her if there's anything in her charts that can map the disintegration of the Jewish psyche due to centuries of persecution?!

IN ENGLISH:

HORNIG: Is he often this . . . angry? Does he exhibit feelings of paranoia?

Of course, a brief period of seclusion in Upstate New York might be just the thing. It is so beautiful in the spring! Would you both please wait a moment while I consult with my nurse—

(Dr. Hornig exits quickly.)

IN YIDDISH:

MADJE: She wants to commit you.

Come home with me. You can rest at home. I'll go with you to a rehearsal. It will cheer up the troupe to see you!

And then we'll be able to go to the Apollo Theatre for our opening night.

(*Hand in hand, they run to their box for opening night.*)

"AIN'T WE GOT FUN" (INSTRUMENTAL REPRISE)

1923, ON BROADWAY:

A LESSON IN LOVE

THE ADDING MACHINE

THE MAN WHO MARRIED A DUMB WIFE

RED LIGHT ANNIE

THE WOMAN ON THE JURY

SALOME

OEDIPUS REX

A NIGHT OF LOVE

THE CHERRY ORCHARD

THE POT BOILER

THE LOWER DEPTHS

IN THE NEXT ROOM

THE GOD OF VENGEANCE (THE FIRST KISS BETWEEN TWO WOMEN ON BROADWAY)

1923: OPENING NIGHT ON BROADWAY, INTERMISSION

ASCH: My God.

MADJE: Those aren't minor changes. Oh, Sholem.

ASCH: I—I feel sick to my stomach. My God.

MADJE: Why are there so many police in the house?

ASCH: It's nothing.

MADJE: I've never attended a Broadway opening before. So are you saying this is what they do uptown?

47

ASCH: You know we've had threats.

MADJE: There were threats downtown. We never had any police downtown.

ASCH: Nobody paid attention because we were downtown.

MADJE: Are they going to stop the show? Because of the lesbianism? Because of the Torah? Because of the prostitution?

ASCH: Because I'm Jewish. We're polack kikes! On Broadway.

(Asch tries to find control.)

I gotta find Harry. I'm going backstage . . . try to look like you're enjoying it.

Beginning of Act Three

Onstage:

SARAH: These things happen. Manke is opening a whorehouse of her own—with our daughter!

We bought a Torah to keep her pure. We can buy her back. Wait— *(She takes off her earrings)* The diamond earrings Yekel gave me, these'll do the trick—

I will be back with our daughter. If I have to drag her by the hair through the streets.

(As Sarah hurries through the streets:)

And if we pull this off, and we buy her a husband, then what? A boy who is scared to look at her, who prays for his sins if he happens to see her flesh and he, God forbid, becomes stiff . . .

But then she meets an older girl. Who is rough on the edges. Who promises her soft things. And Manke knows

48

how to brush on the rouge, how to stand in the light, how to touch Rifkele's hair so lightly, like a feather, like silk . . .
These things . . . happen. Well. *(She adjusts her wig)*
No squelching once the ketubah is signed. What are we selling to the buyer?
Tissue. A thin strip of flesh, a spot of blood, a pinch, and it's over.
Our daughter. A deal is a deal.

(Offstage.
Spotlight on Officer Benjamin Bailie of the 4th Precinct. Vice Squad.
He watches the confrontation between Sarah, Manke and Rifkele intently.
Sarah threatens. Rifkele resists and clings to Manke. And then, Manke lets Rifkele go.
The lovers part. Sarah roughly hauls her daughter out of bed.)

Officer Bailie Enters the Wings

Lemml stands at the ready for the curtain, watching the last moments of the play. Sholem Asch waits. Officer Bailie softly comes behind Lemml.

LEMML: Sir?

BAILIE: I'm Officer Bailie with the 4th Precinct. Vice Squad. And you are?

LEMML: I'm the stage manager of this play. We got a cue coming up here, Officer.

BAILIE: They told me to wait until the end of the play. Who is this?

LEMML: That's the playwright, Sholem Asch. He wrote the play.

BAILIE: Boy, Mr. Asch, I'd like to spend a night in your mind. *(To Lemml)* Will you ask the company to meet me here when the play is over?

LEMML (*Softly*): I will do whatever the law asks me to do, Officer. But I got a cue coming.

ASCH: Are we arrest?

LEMML: We got a cue coming.

BAILIE: I don't have a warrant for you, Mr. Asch. Just the actors.

(*They listen to the last scene of the play. Pause.*)

A BLINK IN TIME

The Last Moments on Broadway

Onstage:

SARAH: Come in. Come in. Your father won't beat you.

YEKEL: Don't be afraid, I won't beat you. Don't be afraid.

RIFKELE: Why should I be afraid?

YEKEL: Rifkele. You ran away with Manke last night. Don't tell me where she took you.

　　Daughter, just tell me: Are you still a virgin? . . . Let me see right into your eyes!! Right into your eyes!

RIFKELE: I don't know.

YEKEL: What do you mean—you don't know! Are you still a—

RIFKELE: Oh, but it's all right for you to do? I know who you are and what you do!

YEKEL: I'll tell you what you know. You know what this Torah cost? It cost all of the whores downstairs on their backs and their knees for a year! And for what? Look at me. God wants me to fail as a father? As a husband? Well there's one thing I know how to do—MAKE MONEY. You are both paying me back! On your backs. On your knees. Down into the whorehouse with you!

SARAH: Help, he's going crazy!

YEKEL: And take the Holy Scroll with you! I don't need it anymore!

Cast and Producer Arrested for Obscenity

Rabbi Joseph Silverman appears on a pulpit. He straightens his beautiful suit. Lemml and Asch remain frozen at the curtain.

IN ENGLISH:

SILVERMAN: And so every time I pick up the paper and I read about:
> A robber who assaults an eighty-year-old grandmother—
> A mother who was at a bar when a fire broke out and consumed all of her children at home—
> Men who were caught together in the park in the light of day—
> I lift my face to the heavens and I pray, please, oh Lord, please do not let them be Jewish!
> This is what it means to be Jewish in America.

Rabbi Silverman—A Sermon, Temple Emanu-El

SILVERMAN: Each day we struggle to uplift the wretched refuse who huddle ten to a room on the Lower East Side, aware of our American duty and privilege as Jews who have long called these shores our home. We advocate day and night that the restriction on the so-called polack, litvak, greenhorn!—that these quotas be lifted so that those unfortunates of our faith can escape the massacres spreading through Europe.

But none of us can live in a constant vigilance. And so perhaps we go to the theater for a little relief, to be in a community that laughs together—

And what is in the theater? What title glares its name in neon lights on Broadway?

The God of Vengeance! By Sholem Asch!

I expect scurrilous lies to my face from the crackpots who call themselves Christian—but to be hit by a stone in my back by a fellow Jew!

I am not unaware that there is a Jewish underground in our cities. Yes, there are girls who, in fleeing Vilna, Kiev, Galicia, without father or family, ply their flesh to buy their daily bread. Are there misguided girls among them who turn to each other in confusion? Of course.

Yes there are men who buy their bread on the sweat of these women's backs, rather than the honorable sweat of their own. Of these parasites I say: Send them back.

I know you have heard me denounce this play before. I acted on my words. I registered the complaint. And I am happy to tell you that as of last night, the play has been closed down by the Vice Squad, and all cast members have been arrested for obscenity.

Please join with me in prayer for a righteous verdict. It is now in the hands of an American jury. We ask that they defend our good name.

AFTER A NIGHT IN JAIL

Lemml and Reina stand anxiously outside the jail.
Esther exits, sees them, and quickly puts on bravado.

IN YIDDISH:

REINA: Esther!

ESTHER: Hello my girl. Oh Reina, We've missed you.

LEMML: I have been so worried . . . I asked that young Cossack to take me too, but he didn't want nothing of me.

REINA: Are they keeping Deine?

ESTHER: Harry was paying her bail when I left. She'll be right behind me.

LEMML: Miss McFadden's father sent a fancy-shmancy lawyer and she's on her way to North Carolina.

ESTHER: When the going gets tough, the goyim get goin'.

(Reina goes over to the jail's entrance and waits.)

Last night the Vice Squad rounded up girls in the cathouses who hadn't paid up, so around three, four A.M. all these girls was pouring in. When I told the ladies I was a thespian, there was a lot of jokes the rest of the night. Ah, sticks and bones.

They was all American girls. Some of their words weren't so dainty, but their English was perfect.

Lou, in my head, I can hear those English words so good . . . But then when I open my mouth, it's like the dust of Poland is in my throat.

(Dorothee enters. She runs to Reina.)

DOROTHEE: I didn't think you would come.

REINA: I couldn't sleep when Lou called me. Did you get any sleep?

DOROTHEE: I haven't slept in weeks. Not since I left your bed.

REINA: Come home with me . . . I said some things I should not have said.

DOROTHEE: You said the truth. I would not be ashamed to be arrested for acting in the play I believed in. I am ashamed I acted in this sham I don't believe in.

REINA: You wanted to be on Broadway.

(Reina sees Dorothee scratching herself.)

Why are you?—

DOROTHEE: —Bedbugs. You still want me in your bed?

IN ENGLISH:

REINA: —Oh! . . . We are going go home. We will stand
together on th-the-shvel.

DOROTHEE: Threshold.

REINA: Threshold of our home. First you take clothes off. All.
And then I take off. All.
So then I wash them. The clothes.

DOROTHEE: Oh.

REINA: Then for you I make a chhh-hot bath, we get in th-th-
vane /

DOROTHEE: Bathtub—

REINA: In our kitchen. You lean against me and I wash your
cchayrr . . . And den we see ch-what will happen.

DOROTHEE: Reina? . . . mamelushn.

EUGENE O'NEILL AT THE HELL HOLE, A WEST VILLAGE BAR

*Lemml stands in a dark bar, The Hell Hole, beside Eugene O'Neill,
Pulitzer Prize–winning playwright of* Anna Christie. *O'Neill is only
into his first drink.*

O'NEILL: Sorry if some of the fellas got rough on you. They
tagged you for a Prohibition Agent hell-bent on breaking
our bottles.

LEMML: I'm a stage manager. *The God of Vengeance.*

O'NEILL: You could use a drink then.

(*O'Neill motions to the bartender. Some dark substance in a glass
is placed on the bar.*)

The finest spirit you can find south of Canada. It does the trick. Drink up.

(O'Neill belts it back. Lemml tries, and gasps.)

What can I do for you—

LEMML: —Lou. I just want to say, Mr. O'Neill, what an honor it is for me—

(O'Neill belts down number two.)

—And congratulations on the Pulitzer for your play *Anna Christie*. Thank you for being willing to testify for our production—

O'NEILL: Oh hell, wish I could have. It's a corker of a play.

LEMML: What happened in the courtroom just now? You left before I could ask—

O'NEILL: The court dismissed all the defense witnesses— We are all barred from testifying. You all are up the shite's creek without a paddle.

LEMML: Why?

O'NEILL: So your Mr. Asch and your play itself isn't on trial for obscenity—the production is.

LEMML: Yessir. But why—

O'NEILL: I couldn't testify to the wholesome and morally fortifying nature of this production because I saw it downtown at the Provincetown Players. They say the script may have been tampered with on its way uptown.

LEMML: Oh.

O'NEILL: Was the script changed from when I saw it?

LEMML: It was.

O'NEILL: Goddamn Harry! Look he's a smart lawyer—he's my lawyer!—but he doesn't know his rising action from his purgation. Look, your only chance now, as I see it, is to get

Mr. Asch on that defense stand in behalf of his play. He has to explain some basic things: that when we trade our souls for money, it's a long and lonely life without love.

(O'Neill motions for another shot. He is pensive, then he shoots it back.)

Your Mr. Asch is a fierce moralist. They're gonna claim they're closing it because of *Homo sexualis*. That's bunk. They're closing it because the play shows that every religion—even Jews—sell God for a price. Give my admiration to Mr. Asch. He's crafted a play that shrouds us in a deep, deep fog of human depravity: then like a lighthouse, those two girls. That's a beacon I will remember.

(O'Neill pays up.)

Tell him to keep his head down, don't take any shots to his kidneys—then up, up, a left jab, right hook combination!

LEMML *(Totally lost)*: Yessir.

O'NEILL: Better luck on his next play.

LEMML: Oh, Mr. Asch doesn't write plays anymore—only novels.

O'NEILL: Smart man. Oh—the stage—I wish I could quit it! "Dat ole davil sea make dem crazy fools with her dirty tricks! It's so!"

(O'Neill lurches from The Hell Hole. Lemml watches him leave.)

STATEN ISLAND: SHOLEM AND MADJE ASCH'S HOME

FROM NOW ON, ONLY IN YIDDISH:

Sholem Asch, slumped over his typewriter, pretends to write.

IN YIDDISH:

MADJE: Husband. That was Lemml on the phone.

ASCH: I'm trying to write! It's like a goddamn circus down here with you and the children.

MADJE: The children and I tiptoe around here like it's a goddamn museum. You have got to call him back. This is Lemml. He worships you. You just can't discard people.

The court has thrown out all the defense witnesses.

I've laid out your clothes. You need to change. We have to catch the ferry in a half hour.

(They start dressing him.)

ASCH: This is a nightmare.

MADJE: Harry will translate what you say if he has to.

ASCH: Like he translated my play?

MADJE: You just have to make an appearance in the courtroom.

ASCH: There are massacres right now all over Europe!! And I'm supposed to care about what I wrote when I was in short pants?

MADJE: It's still a very important play.

ASCH: Madje. I can't. I just can't.

(Asch is now dressed. He sits on the bed.
Pause.)

MADJE: I wish you had never gone to Vilna. I wish you would tell me what you saw.

ASCH: I don't want you to know. You're my wife.

Everything is reversed now: like a photographic negative. Our garden, our house, the theater, the streets in America feel very far away. What's real to me—vivid to me—

I can't get the images out of my head. It's hard for me to kiss our children at night. And when as head of our delegation I reported all the atrocities I saw what is the response from our State Department? . . . These things happen.

MADJE: . . . I think you should tell your friends that you are struggling with this. Tell Lemml. He's wondering where you are.

ASCH: I have to put myself together. I don't want people to know I am sitting in my house, weeping.

Will you call Lemml?

MADJE: Of course.

ASCH: I'll write a letter to the court.

MADJE: Yes. Your words are powerful.

ASCH: I have to write something to change the way gentiles see us—that make them see that we are one people with one common root—or they will rip us out, root by root, from the earth until we are no more.

It's coming. It's coming here.

MADJE: No. It won't happen here. We're safe here.

1923, THE VERDICT: PEOPLE OF THE STATE OF NEW YORK VS. THE GOD OF VENGEANCE

JUDGE MCINTYRE: The defendants have been found guilty of presenting an indecent, obscene, and immoral play, exhibition and drama. Although the theatrical profession is not as exalted as the other literary arts, this judgment still signals that the People of New York State are entitled to morally upright, wholesome American drama. The time has come when the drama must be purified of Eastern exoticism, its sexual pollution and its corruptive attitude towards the family. Court dismissed.

Lemml Watches the Sun Rise Over Staten Island

The sun is just streaking the sky. Madje, in a robe and slippers, unlocks the back door to get the milk. Sitting there on the porch, quietly, his knees up to his chest, is Lemml. He gently holds up the bottles of milk and cream.

A short scream from Madje.

IN YIDDISH:

LEMML: Sorry Mrs. Madje. We don't want to disturb your husband.

MADJE: Oh my god, Lemml! I didn't expect— *(She takes the bottles from him)* Are you all right?

LEMML: I been better. The world spins on.

MADJE: How long have you been here?

LEMML *(Shrugs)*: I wanted to see what the sunrise was like from Staten Island.

MADJE: Come in. Come in, Lemml. I am putting on the coffee.

LEMML: No. Thank you, I do not want to step over your shvel.

MADJE: Oh Lemml. Please. Please come in.

LEMML: I might be a dybbuk. A dead soul inside a stage manager.

(Asch appears in pants, shirt and sweater. He stands in his threshold. Lemml does not turn to him.

Madje goes in, leaving the door open. A moment. Lemml watches the sun rise over Staten Island.

With false heartiness:)

ASCH: Lemml! My good man! Please come in.

LEMML: I don't think I am your good man anymore, Mr. Asch.

ASCH: Well, then, may I join you?

LEMML: Please yourself.

(Asch sits on the porch beside Lemml.)

The time to join me was yesterday. Or the day before. That
was the time to join me.

ASCH: I owe you an apology.

LEMML: You owe me nothing. *(Beat)* The letter you wrote to the
court was very beautiful. You got powerful words, Mr. Asch.

ASCH: I know you think of me as the young firebrand you saw
the night we met.
Every day since the day we read it out loud, I have been
under attack. —Mr. Peretz was right—the play is a stone.

LEMML: I didn't expect you to defend this play. I expected you
to defend us. Do you know, Mr. Asch, that this play has
ended Mr. Schildkraut's chance at the great roles in theater? He will never get the chance on an American stage
again.

ASCH: He is a giant on the stages of Europe.

LEMML: If he stays in this country, the best he can hope for on
American stages is to play the "Stage Jew."

ASCH: At least he'll make a living. None of you will be out of
work in—

(Lemml rises.)

LEMML: —How dare you! We are not doing your play for the
money! I could make as much wid' my sewing!
Why did you agree to those cuts? You cut the love
between those two girls. There's only sex left!

(Madje appears with coffee.)

ASCH: I told Harry and Rudolph to do what they want. It's my
play!

MADJE: And mine. It's my play too.

LEMML: Excuse me, Mrs., but the play belongs to the people who labor in it! And the audience who put aside the time to be there in person!

ASCH: The truth is—I never checked the cuts. I can barely read English. I can barely speak! A writer of world literature— I couldn't walk into that court, I couldn't walk into that court—in front of all those American reporters— they would laugh at me! Can you imagine if I opened my mouth? I would sound just like you.

IN ENGLISH:

LEMML: I am done being in a country that laughs at the way I speak. They say America is free? What do you know here is free? All over Europe we did this play with no Cossacks shutting us down. Berlin, Moscow, Odessa—everywhere there is theater! You don't have the money for a ticket? Tickets over there cost less than a cup of tea. Then you dress up nice in your best coat and maybe you stand up in the second gallery, but you can say to your grandchildren: "I saw the great Rudolph Schildkraut in Sholem Asch's *The God of Vengeance!*"
     I am leaving this country.

ASCH: Oh, no no no please—   MADJE: Lemml, the places you
                                        still care for have changed . . .

LEMML: —You have washed your hands clean of this tailor from Balut! Who doesn't stand up for the name on his title page? I am taking the manuscript in Yiddish wid me.
     (*Geshray*) Mr. Asch! Your play it changed my life—
ASCH: Lemml: Listen, wait—
MADJE: Wait, Lemml —
LEMML: I am going home.

A BLINK IN TIME

Lemml starts his return back to Poland.

As Lemml continues his trek (a long, heavy, slow journey), the audience becomes a well-fed American audience in the Catskills. We would never know there's a war going on thousands of miles away. As our songbirds warble:

1938, STATEN ISLAND: SHOLEM ASCH IN HIS STUDY

SELECTED WORKS OF SHOLEM ASCH:

A SHTETL

WITH THE CURRENT

THE MESSIANIC ERA

THE GOD OF VENGEANCE

SABBATAI ZEVI

UNCLE MOSES

MOTKE THE THIEF

KIDDUSH HA-SHEM

BEFORE THE DELUGE

THE SAYER OF PSALMS

THE NAZARENE

THE APOSTLE

MARY

EAST RIVER

THE PROPHET

Lemml returns home. Asch types furiously.

1938, GROSSINGER'S CATSKILLS RESORT: THE BAGELMAN SISTERS

"BEI MIR BIST DU SHEYN"

Chana, a Bagelman Sister, sings "Bei Mir Bist Du Sheyn":

CHANA:
> Of all the boys I've known and I've known some
> Until I first met you I was lonesome
> And when you came in sight, dear, my heart grew light
> And this old world seemed new to me.

(Halina, a Bagelman Sister, sings:)

HALINA:
> You're really swell I have to admit you
> Deserve expressions that really fit you
> And so I've racked my brain, hoping to explain
> All the things that you do to me.

(Halina and Chana sing:)

HALINA AND CHANA:
> Bei mir bist du sheyn, please let me explain,
> Bei mir bist du sheyn, means that you're grand
> Bei mir bist du sheyn, again I'll explain
> It means you're the fairest in the land.
>
> I could say, "Bella, Bella," even say, "Voonderbar,"
> Each language only helps me tell you how grand you are!

1939: Nakhmen Rehearses

NAKHMEN: I would like to speak to the French Ambassador.

(He practices his French:)

Pardonnez-moi: Je voudrais parler à l'ambassadeur.

(Beat. Take two:)

Pardonnez-moi: Je voudrais parler à l'ambassadeur.

(Nervous, Nakhmen combs his hair, sits, and waits.)

The Ararat Theatre Troupe, Krakowa Street

Halina sings:

HALINA:
Kh'vel dir zogn, dir glaykh tzu hern
Az du zolst mir libe derklern
Ven du redst mit di oygn
Volt ikh mit dir gefloygn
Vi di vilst, s'art mikh nit.

The French Embassy in Poland

NAKHMEN: Excuse me, do you speak Yiddish?

CHANA *(Sings)*:	NAKHMEN:
Ven du host a bisele seykhl	Hebrew? Polish? Un peu?
Un ven du vaytzt dayn	I would like to talk to the
kindershn shmeykhl	ambassador. I'm sure he's

Vendu bist vild vi an
Amerikaner
Bist afile a Galitsianer
Zog ikh: dos art mikh nit.

HALINA (Sings):
Bei mir bist du sheyn,
Bei mir hos tu kheyn,
Bei mir bist du eyner oyf
der velt.
Bei mir bist du eyner oyf
der velt.
Bei mir bist du eyner oyf
der velt.
Bei mir bist du eyner oyf
der velt.

busy. He will want to make
time for me. I am a Yiddish
writer well-known throughout Europe ... I come from
Warsaw. Yes. Varsovie.
What? Do I know Sholem
Asch. (Irritated) Of course!
I gave him notes in the
salon during the first
reading of The God of—
would you please ask if
I might talk to the—

1939–1941: LETTERS FROM POLAND

Asch is still typing furiously. The troupe stands behind him.

VERA: Dear Madje, dear Sholem: We opened *The God of Vengeance* last night to thunderous applause!

CHANA: Thank you so much for the opening night care package!—

HALINA: Thank you so much for the new book, I love your novels!

NAKHMEN: Pardonnez-moi: Je voudrais parler à l'ambassadeur!

OTTO: The authorities are cramming in Jews from Germany into every spare inch of space.

NAKHMEN: Peut-être avez-vous entendu parler de moi! Sholem Asch has said that I was an inspiration for—

VERA: —Dear Sholem: You must tell your wife, my dearest friend in all the world, that I feel rich! I have a warm coat and a little food.

NAKHMEN (*Cheerfully*): Mais oui! Sholem Asch! Sholem!

OTTO: The authorities have walled us into the old Balut district to the north.

HALINA: I can still see the city park across the street!

NAKHMEN: Sholem Asch est un ami proche!

CHANA: We are still performing *The God of Vengeance* in all kinds of spaces:

VERA: basements,

HALINA: cafés,

CHANA: the lobby of the old children's hospital—

OTTO: The authorities forbid us to perform plays!

VERA: Good-bye Shakespeare!

CHANA: Chekhov!

HALINA: George Bernard Shaw!—

OTTO: Songs, dances, skits only six nights a week! Nakhmen is learning French.

NAKHMEN: Il n'y a plus de visas?!

HALINA: Oh Mrs. Asch, I most of all want to lie in the grass again!—

CHANA: —To smell the grass!

VERA: Nakhmen is learning Spanish!

NAKHMEN: ¡Españolas damas son la más bella—por favor! ¿La embajada está cerrada?

OTTO: Nakhmen is learning Chinese!

NAKHMEN: Qing! Qing!—búyào guān dàmén! I have been waiting for three days in a very long line. —Please! Do not close the gates before I—

(*A beat.*)

My dear Asch, it has been a long time since we read your brilliant little play in the living room. A lot of Yiddish water has flowed over the Polish dam. It is hard for me to ask you: The authorities have confiscated our passports. Is there any way you might put in a word to the consulate to make an exception for me?

(Asch rips out the page in his typewriter and puts in a new sheet. He types:)

ASCH: Lemml, I hope I may still call myself your friend.
  My letters to you have all been "returned to sender." If you get this, will you please respond?

A BLINK IN TIME

The troupe enters a dusty space.

LEMML: All right, people! This will make a stage!

(The lights grow stronger. The troupe organizes some jumbled benches. They carry on suitcases. They work. In the corner of the attic, they find a horsehair sofa with its guts spilling out.)

CHANA: Lemml, can we use this?
LEMML: Mrs. Gitla won't mind. Chana, this will be the sitting room . . . Halina, over here the stairs . . .
VERA: Here's the curtain for Miss Manke's place of business.
LEMML: Yes! Vera, excellent.
MENDEL: Let's hang the lamps! Matches? Lemml?
LEMML: Mendel! Don't waste a single match.

(Avram begins to sweep.)

Avram, let me do that. You get ready.

(Otto returns.)

Otto? Do we have an audience?

OTTO: A few souls . . .

(The troupe starts.)

AVRAM: Let's hope they brought some food.

OTTO: Or some money.

(A projected title begins to flicker on the screen.)

LEMML: Okay, people, may I have your attention please, everyone draw near. Five minutes to Act Two. We are a . . .
few players . . . we are missing a few of the cast. Chana.
Remember to keep your shawl on over your hair when you
are playing one of the working girls downstairs. Mendel,
Avram—you wear the shawls when you play the girls.

(Mendel drapes a shawl over his head.)

MENDEL AND AVRAM: Yes, darling!

LEMML: So Chana, when you enter as Rifkele—

CHANA: Without the shawl.

LEMML: And Halina? Are you feeling strong enough? —Then
you play Manke tonight, and Manke only. We are not wet-
ting the shawls in the rain scene. Okay? I will read the stage
directions. As it is, in your nightgown, you can catch your
death of cold—

HALINA: I'm fine.

(The projected title now comes into focus:)

1943, ŁÓDŹ GHETTO, POLAND:
AN ATTIC TURNED INTO A STAGE

LEMML: All right, people.

(Lemml opens up another suitcase and draws out an entire loaf of black market bread. There is a gasp.)

VERA: I could veyn!

HALINA: Lemml!

LEMML: Esn! Everyone, take some, take some.

(The troupe breaks off big hunks and carefully distributes.)

OTTO: Shall I let them in?

(Lemml nods.)

Places for the Act Two.

A BLINK IN TIME

Lemml steps into the light.

LEMML: Ladies, gentlemen. Let's have a round of applause for our band: Making the clarinet wail, we have Mr. Mayer Balsam! *(Bow)* On violin, our very own Miss Nelly Friedman! *(Bow)* And on accordion, the dexterous Mr. Moriz Godowsky! *(Bow)* Welcome to our show tonight. As you know, six nights a week we gather together to sing songs we know and love, to dance, to escape our daily lives. But on the seventh night . . . God created Yiddish theater. First, let me give our thanks to Mrs. Gitla Bronowski for letting us use this spacious attic for our show (*A smattering of applause*) Thank you, Mrs. Gitla! Tonight we are going to perform Act Two of the greatest play ever written by one of our countrymen, Sholem Asch. *The God of Vengeance.* As you all know, as a young man I was privileged to hear the first reading of this masterpiece in Warsaw, and it changed my life.

Last week we presented Act One, and God willing, next week we will still be here to perform Act Three.

Does anyone here need to know what happens in the first act? So you know last week Act One happened upstairs in Yekel's living room,

Tonight takes place in another location in Yekel's house: the cellar.

Manke, the star of his stable, is forming a friendship— yes? With the daughter. Okay, that's all we need to know.

Speaking of gelt . . . should tonight's performance so move you, we would appreciate any contribution . . . a mark or two, any food you may be able to spare . . . And if our performance does not please you, please throw food! Kugel! Rugelach, anyone? We have made slight cuts to the script so we do not break curfew. And in tonight's performance, in the role of Manke, played so brilliantly the last few years by our own Ada Borenstein . . . Halina Cygansky is stepping in tonight. To set the scene: It's late night in the ghetto. And it's raining. Without further ado, *The God of Vengeance.* Act Two.

The Rain Scene

Manke softly taps for Rifkele.

MANKE: Rifkele, Rifkele . . .

RIFKELE: Manke, Manke . . . did you call me?

MANKE: Yes, Rifkele. Come, we'll stand in the May rain, splash water over each other and get wet down to our skin.

RIFKELE: Shhh. Speak softly.

MANKE: I'll loosen your hair. I want to wash your hair in the rain.

RIFKELE: I heard you tapping and I tiptoed out so quietly Papa couldn't hear me.

MANKE: The night is so beautiful, the rain is so fresh and everything is so sweet in this air.

RIFKELE: Shhh, shhh. My father beat me.

MANKE: He won't hurt you anymore.

They Feel the Rain

Manke leads Rifkele into a flood of light. They turn their faces up to the light. They feel the rain. They reenter the brothel wrapped in their shawls. Manke leads Rifkele to the sofa.

MANKE: Are you shivering, Rifkele?

RIFKELE: I'm cold.

MANKE: Let me wrap my body around you.

RIFKELE: —That's nice.

MANKE: Oh, You smell like grass in the meadows . . . you let me wash your breasts in the rain.

RIFKELE: I did.

MANKE: Your breasts are so pale. So soft.

RIFKELE: Manke. I want you to teach me.

MANKE: Wait, wait . . . let me brush your hair—like a bride's hair with two long braids. Do you want me to Rifkele, do you want us to . . . ?

RIFKELE: Yes. Yes.

MANKE: You are my bride—you take my breath away! We sit at the shabbes table after your parents have gone to sleep.

We're alone. And we're shy. But you are my bride and I am your bridegroom.

RIFKELE: I want you to take me.

MANKE: Are you sure?

(Beat.)

RIFKELE: I want to taste you.

(They kiss.)

MANKE: Isn't it good, Rifkele? Isn't it good?

RIFKELE: God yes.

MANKE: Now we lie together in one bed. No one will see. Would you like to stay with me all night in one bed?

RIFKELE: I do. I do.

MANKE: I can't breathe. Come to me. Come to me.

(Suddenly there is the sound offstage of a door being kicked open; and the terrifying sound of boots running up the stairs. The troupe knows the time has come.)

CHANA: I'm scared.

A BLINK IN TIME
A BLINK IN TIME . . .

The troupe forms a single-file line. We have come to our Kaddish. "Wiegala" was written by Ilse Weber, a nurse at the Children's Hospital at Theresienstadt. She sang this lullaby for the children in the wards. When it came time for the children to be transported to Auschwitz, Ilse volunteered to go with them. It is said she sang this song in line to the chambers: "The wind plays on the lyre, the nightingale sings, the moon is a lantern . . . sleep, my little child, sleep."

"WIEGALA"

Halina and Chana sing "Wiegala":

HALINA AND CHANA:
Vigala, Vigala, Vayer
Der Vind shpilt aufder Layer.
Ir shpilt tzu zis im grunen Rid
Di Nachtigal, di zing ir Lid.
Vigala, Vigala, Vayer
Der Vind shpilt aufder Layer.

AN IMPOSSIBLY LONG
LINE
THE SMELL OF SMOKE
AND ASH IS THICK
IN THE AIR.
THEN THE WIND
SHIFTS DIRECTION.

Vigala, Vigala, Verne
Der Mond is di Lanterne
Ir shtit am dunklen
Himeltzelt
Und shout hernider auf di Velt.
Vigala, Vigala, Verne
Der Mond is di Lanterne.

THE TROUPE CAN
SMELL
THE GRASS IN THE
MEADOW.

LEMML CLOSES HIS
EYES.
HE MAKES A WISH.

LEMML *(Softly)*: Please don't let this be the ending . . .

IN HIS MIND, ONLY HE CAN SEE . . .

RIFKELE AND MANKE BURST OUT OF THE LINE.

THEY ESCAPE.

LEMML OPENS HIS EYES.

Ashes to Ashes: The Troupe Returns to Dust

A BLINK IN TIME

Oklahoma *plays on a record player. It is very loud. The troupe stares into the audience, and as the music plays:*

Very Few Write in Yiddish Anymore

1952, Bridgeport, Connecticut: Moving Day, Sholem and Madje Asch's House

Madje enters an empty room with two suitcases.

IN YIDDISH:

MADJE: Everything's packed up. Once we get to London we'll tell them where to send the furniture. We'll have a nice visit with our daughter. We'll figure it out.

ASCH: We could just leave it. Everything.

(*Beat.*)

MADJE: I told that nice young man to come by for a quick visit before we left.

ASCH: Who?

MADJE: The one who is producing your play.

ASCH: Now?!

MADJE: We are inviting him over our shvel while we still have one.

(A tapping at the door.)

That's him.

ASCH: Rome is burning and you want to put on a play!

MADJE: Rome is always burning! Last night you said you'd consider it. Sholem.

Just give him a moment of your time.

ASCH: I am beside myself with anticipation.

MADJE: Be nice.

(Madje ushers in a young man, John Rosen.)

ROSEN: Thank you, Mrs. Asch, I won't keep your husband long.

(Madje, with a warm smile, exits.)

Mr. Asch. I just want to say what a great honor this is for me.

ASCH: So you are a lover of Yiddish literature, Mr.—?

ROSEN: John Rosen. John. My grandparents speak Yiddish, but my parents—

ASCH: Your parents wanted you to grow up American. This story I have heard. Madje tells me that you got into Yale! It is easier for a camel he should go through the eye of a needle than a Jew he should enter the kingdom of Yale! . . . Madje has read your new translation of the play. I have not. She tells me it is good.

ROSEN: I brought you the most recent copy. I know I am young, but . . . I am starting a new theater company for the great classic works of the stage that ask urgent moral questions!

ASCH: In Connecticut? Well good luck with that, young man!

ROSEN: *The God of Vengeance* has the urgency of today! —I want to bring it to American audiences just as you wrote it—

ASCH: Young man: I have to tell you—I no longer care what is done on the stages of this country. Theater companies are started by young men who have the luxury to care about where they live. Or the false belief that they will be allowed to live in the place they care about.

(*Asch brings out a letter from his jacket pocket.*)

A little invite from the Congress. The House of the Un-American Activities. In 1905 I was attracted by socialists. We are all brothers! Ale brider!

ROSEN: Mr. Asch! You must fight this!

ASCH: Mr. John—have you ever lost audience members? Did you watch them walk up the aisle in the middle of your play?

ROSEN: Yes! That's happened to me all the time at Yale. Townspeople fleeing up the aisles!

ASCH: Ach. I too have lost audience members. Six million have left the theater. I am sorry to waste your time. (*Upset*) I will not let this play be produced. No more. I wrote it in a different time. The time has changed on me. (*Beat*) You must excuse me—the way out you know.

(*Rosen, stunned, stands, then moves toward the door. Asch calls out:*)

In the words of a much wiser man—if I was you, burn it!

ROSEN: Mr. Asch: I may have to wait many many years—but I am producing your play!

(*Rosen shuts the door behind him. Asch stands in silence. Beat. He picks up the two suitcases and starts to exit.*
The ghost of Lemml stands in his way.
Asch suddenly turns back into the room. And there in his empty living room it starts to rain. The dead troupe rises to join him, watching from the wings.
He remembers:)

MANKE: Rifkele, Rifkele— Di nakht iz azoy lib, der regn iz azoy frish, un alts shmekt azoy in der luft.

RIFKELE: Shvayg, shvayg. Der tate hot mikh geshlogn. Er hot di shtib tsugeshlosn, un hot dem shlisl bahaltn—

MANKE: Er vet dikh keynmol mer nisht vey tin.

(As Rifkele and Manke dance in the rain, Lemml and Asch join them.)

END

PAULA VOGEL is the Pulitzer Prize–winning author of *How I Learned to Drive.* Her other plays include *The Long Christmas Ride Home, Don Juan Comes Home from Iraq, The Mineola Twins, The Baltimore Waltz, Hot 'N' Throbbing, Desdemona, And Baby Makes Seven, The Oldest Profession,* and *A Civil War Christmas.* Upcoming projects include her play *No Place Like* and the book *How to Bake a Play.* Her numerous awards include the Pulitzer Prize for Drama, an Obie Award for Lifetime Achievement, the New York Drama Critics' Circle Award, the Lifetime Achievement in the American Theater Award from the Theater Hall of Fame, the Award for Literature from the American Academy of Arts and Letters, and a Lily Award, among many others. She is honored by the awards given in her name from the American Theatre College Festival, Philadelphia Young Playwrights, and the Vineyard Theatre. After teaching for more than thirty years at Brown University and the Yale School of Drama, she now conducts workshops at theaters, schools, and community organizations. She is a member of the Dramatists Guild.

*Theatre Communications Group would like to offer our special
thanks to Paula Marie Black for her generous support of
the publication of* Indecent *by Paula Vogel*

PAULA MARIE BLACK is a Drama Desk, Drama League,
Tony Award, Olivier Award, and Helpmann Award–
winning producer dedicating her efforts in theatre to women
directors, playwrights, and all people who have not had a voice.

Women's Voices in the Art of Theatre is an endowment
that Paula established in perpetuity at La Jolla Playhouse,
benefitting women as directors, playwrights, and book writers of musicals.

TCG books sponsored by Paula include:

Annie Baker, *John*
Amy Herzog, *The Great God Pan* and *Belleville*
Lynn Nottage, *Sweat*
Suzan-Lori Parks, *The Book of Grace*
Paula Vogel, *Indecent*

THEATRE COMMUNICATIONS GROUP (TCG), the national
organization for the American theatre, promotes the idea of
"A Better World for Theatre, and a Better World Because
of Theatre." In addition to TCG's numerous services to the
theatre field, TCG Books is the nation's largest independent
publisher of dramatic literature, with 15 Pulitzer Prizes for
Best Play on its book list. The book program commits to the
life-long career of its playwrights, keeping all of their plays in
print. TCG Books' other authors include: Nilo Cruz, Quiara
Alegría Hudes, David Henry Hwang, Tony Kushner, Don-
ald Margulies, Sarah Ruhl, Stephen Sondheim, Anne Wash-
burn, and August Wilson, among many others.

Support TCG's work in the theatre field by becoming a
member or donor: www.tcg.org